William Brough

Prince Amabel; or, the fairy roses:

An original fairy extravaganza

William Brough

Prince Amabel; or, the fairy roses:
An original fairy extravaganza

ISBN/EAN: 9783337736330

Printed in Europe, USA, Canada, Australia, Japan

Cover: Foto ©ninafisch / pixelio.de

More available books at **www.hansebooks.com**

PRINCE AMABEL;

OR,

THE FAIRY ROSES.

An Original Fairy Extravaganza,

BY

WILLIAM BROUGH

(Member of the Dramatic Authors' Society),

AUTHOR OF

Perseus and Andromeda; Endymion, or the Naughty Boy who Cried for the
Moon; Conrad and Medora; Lalla Rookh; Perdita, the Royal Milk-
maid; Prince Prettypet and the Butterfly; &c. &c.

THOMAS HAILES LACY,
89, STRAND,
(Opposite Southampton Street, Covent Garden Market,)
LONDON.

PRINCE AMABEL.

Scene First.—*Summer Palace of King Buonocore.*

Buonocore, Lord Kootoo, *and* Council *assembled;
flourish of trumpets, as the* King *rises to deliver the
Royal Speech.*

Buonocore. (R.) My lords and gentlemen, I've sum-
    moned you,
  Not that there's anything for you to do;
  But ancient custom, by whose rules we walk,
  Decrees our parliament should meet—and talk.
  Let foreign realms, which wars and despots worry,
  Themselves with business, loans, and budgets flurry;
  In our blest land we only meet together,
  Chiefly to pass remarks upon the weather;
  Talk pretty platitudes which please, not bore—
  Teaching each other how twice two make four;
  Or, if sometimes a sparring match be added,
  'Tis but a friendly one with gloves well padded.

Chorus of Courtiers, *" Happy Land, Happy Land."*

  My lords and gentlemen, I'll trouble you,
  Not to sing songs till I've my speech got through.
  We are at peace with all the world—'tis said of us,
  Indeed, that all the world's a wholesome dread of us.
  Our happy subjects, with a happy king—
  Famed for his happy knack of governing,
  At morn rise happy—happy sleep at night,
  And eat their dinners with a happy-tite.

  Courtiers *sing, " Happy Land, Happy Land."*

  My lords !

Koot. (R.C.) Great king, your speech delights us—still
  Could you contrive to cut it short?
Buon.   I will.
  No state affair, save one, demands our care,
  My son's low state is a sad *state of heir;*

He weeps, he sighs, walks with a mournful slowness ;
You scarce would know his Highness in his lowness!
My only son—my heir apparent! You (*to* KooToo)
Can feel for me; you *air a parent* too.
What ails him?

KOOT.   Love, sir! He oft sees, it seems,
A form of rarest beauty in his dreams ;
Then waking, his rare beauty melts in air.

BUON. So *making herself scarce* as well as rare.
But how to find this girl he dreams about?

KOOT. I have already messengers sent out
To every neighbouring state, with invitations
To a Great Exhibition of all nations—
A Prize Princess Show!

BUON.   Stuff! man; would you treat
Princesses like fat bulls in Baker-street?
Would'st classify and ticket them, you dog,
Like hogs and cattle in a *catal-ogue ?*
At such a proposition they'd be shocked.

KOOT. Not with the marriage market so o'erstocked
As now.

BUON.   Think you they'll còme?

KOOT.   No room for thinking,
They have come like—excuse the phrase—like winking.
But see ; his Highness!

BUON.   Ah ! still in the dumps ;
His eyes o'erflowing like a pair of pumps.

Enter PRINCE AMABEL, L. U. E.

PRINCE. (C.) Unhappy Amabel! oh, cruel fate,
Was ever prince seen in so sad a state?
The idol of my dreams I nowhere can see,
My fancy's idol seems an idle fancy.

BUON. (R.) Desist, my son. This sighing out of place
Ill suits the *scion* of a noble race.
Heir to the royal purple, why thus choose,
'Stead of in purple, to be in the blues.
I don't get angry easily or soon ;
You'll stir me up, though—acting like a spoon.

PRINCE. Father! no more. Say, has my love been found?

BUON. The fairest maids from every country round

We've hither brought.   'Mongst them she may, I
    trust, be.

PRINCE. If you've got *all* the pretty ones, she must be.
    This galaxy of beauty, quick, let's see.

KOOT. (L.) Come in, my beauties.   (*crosses to* R. U. E.)

BUON. (*sitting*, R.)   Fortune grant that he
    The gal-he-lacks, find in the gal-ax-y.

Music.—Enter the PRINCESSES OF ALL NATIONS, R. U. E.

Concerted Piece, " Haste to the Wedding."

KOOT. Come, haste, and a wedding will soon on the
    tapis be.
    Newspaper scribes thus the fact will declare.

BUON. So once more in my kingdom no soul shall un-
    happy be.
    Haste to select them the fortunate fair.

KOOT. (*bringing forward girls*) Here's a princess from
    Spain; here's another from Portugal;
    Here's one pronounced, of Circassia, the cream.

PRINCE. But no, no—they're not the sort o' gal,
    Like the sweet creature I saw in my dream.

KOOT. In the flower of youth—see Killarney's fair Lily,
    The Blue Bell of Scotland, the Rose of Castille——

PRINCE. No flower—rose, lily, or daffydowndilly—
    Can ever take root in my heart, though, I feel.

KOOT. If none you select, you will surely offend 'em all.
    Thus to dismiss them they'll deem a disgrace.

PRINCE. There, go—go—home again send 'em all—
    Tell 'em not one of them suits for the place.
    (*The* PRINCESSES *murmur discontentedly among*
    themselves, L.)

1ST PRIN. It's shameful!

2ND PRIN.   It's disgusting!

3RD PRIN.   Did you ever?

1ST PRIN. Were ever princesses so treated?

3RD PRIN.   Never!

2ND PRIN. I smiled to show my teeth—I wish I'd bit him.

1ST PRIN. I hoped to strike him—now I'd like to hit him.

PRINCE. (C.) Silence those dreadful belles—tell them—
    nay hold—
    Bells always make more noise the more they're toll'd.

BUON. (R.) Ladies, be calm—come, follow me down stairs,
    You've shown your graces, pray don't show your airs.
3RD PRIN. My carriage, please.
2ND PRIN.   My cab!
1ST PRIN.   My dog-cart !
BUON.   Nay,
    Have patience. (*crosses to* L. C.)
PRINCE.   Don't detain the ladies, pray.
    Call carriage, cab and cart—which lady is it
    That, making calls, comes in a *cart de visit ?*

> (*general movement among the girls, discovering an*
> OLD BEGGAR WOMAN, *crouched down upon the*
> *floor in the midst of them*)

KOOT. (R.) What's this? how came this hag our ranks among?
    We want none here but pretty girls and young.
    Be off with you—come——
PRINCE. (C.)   Nay, my lord, for shame.
    She's old and feeble—sit you down, good dame,
    And rest awhile—how can I serve you, speak !
OLD WOM. (L.) A few short minutes' rest is all I seek.
KOOT. Send to the kitchen, then, the beldam old,
    The kitchen's warm—no fear of *kitchin'* cold,
    Or in the attics room for her engage.
PRINCE. How would you like *room-attics* at her age ?
    Here she shall stay. My sorrow's best distractions
    I find in doing charitable actions.
BUON. (R.) His object's good—of that there's not a doubt;
1ST PRIN. (*pointing*) If that's his object, see it carried out.
PRINCE. Do it yourselves, if you her presence wrongs.
1ST PRIN. I wouldn't touch her with a pair of tongs;
    So by your leave—— (*going*)
PRINCE.   Yes, go—I'd be alone;
    You have my leave; by all means take your own.
BUON. Ladies, you hear—no hint could well be stronger;
1ST PRIN. After that *rude hint*, we'll (*h*) *int-rude* no longer:
    You shall repent this treatment of us though,
    Tremble—revenge—et cetera—
PRINCE.   Yes, I know.

> *Music.—Exeunt* PRINCESSES, BUONOCORE, KOOTOO
> *and* LORDS, L. U. E.

PRINCE. I breathe again—those girls sent to the right about;
    But where is she, the maid, I dream each night about?

Song.—Air, "The Dream of Love."

A dream of love, the sweetest dream,
    That e'er could fire a fellow's brain;
Each night have I. With morn's first beam,
    I wake, to find I'm sold again!
The lovely maid I dream about,
    And see so plain, although so fair—
Though wide-awake, I can't find out;
    Yet give her up, I'll not I swear.
        All other boons I'd ask above,
        Give me my dream, the dream I love!

PRINCE. I am alone. Now to resume my sighs;
OLD WOM. Don't, Prince. (*throws off disguise, and apears as Fairy*)
PRINCE. (R.)   What's this? Can I believe my eyes?
FAIRY. (L.) Start not at the old beggar's transformation,
PRINCE. It really beggars all imagination.
FAIRY. 'Twas but a trial of your heart I made;
    Your conduct's proved you worthy of my aid:
    List, then; the woes which now your bosom haunt,
    P'raps, mend I can——
PRINCE.   Then you're no *mend-i-cant.*
FAIRY. I am a fairy;
PRINCE.   So I should have guessed
    By the amount of gauze in which you're dressed.
FAIRY. (*conceitedly*) Is it effective?
                (*turning round to show herself*)
PRINCE.   Yes, by nature's laws,
    There's no effect without sufficient *gauze.*
FAIRY. You've vainly sought the maid of your affection,
    Your own address won't teach you her direction;
    These fairy roses though to her will guide you,
    And when in danger an escape provide you.
PRINCE. Quick, give them me—my task to set about,
    I wait with eagerness, (*calling*) who waits without?

Enter COUNT MUFFIO *and* COUNT SPOONIO, L.

MUFF. What is your Highness' pleasure?

PRINCE.   Hah, my friends,
    Rejoice with me—this day my sorrow ends ;
    The maid I love I've found the way to reach,
    These flow'rs will tell me——
SPOON.   Are they flow'rs of speech ?
FAIRY. Their leaves will counsel you which way to walk.
PRINCE. A flow'r of speech would counsel by its (s)talk.
FAIRY. Pluck off a leaf, and throw it in the air,
    Watch where it flies and follow it with care—
    There lies your path.
PRINCE.   How ! blown by gusts at random ?
FAIRY. *De gustibus*, sir, non est disputandum ;
    Do as I bid—the wind I'll see about.
PRINCE. This moment on my travels I'll set out—
    Adieu, good friends——
MUFF.   Nay, we will go with you,
    About the question pray make no *ado*.
SPOON. The heir apparent's travels we will share,
    As an accompaniment to the *heir*.
PRINCE. Accompany the *heir !* well, get your hats ;
    'Tis an accompaniment in two flats.
FAIRY. One moment more. Should danger overtake you,
    Smell the white rose, invisible 'twill make you ;
    You may go where you will—leap, dance, shout, run,
    Your form will cast no shadow in the sun.
    No sound you make be heard.   Of eyes bereft
    To lookers-on the charm will cry, " eyes left."
    Smelling the red rose you're once more in sight,
    For you 'tis " as you were," for them " eyes right."
    Each rose will serve but once, mind.   Now good-bye.
                        (*disappears suddenly*, L. U. E.)
PRINCE. She's gone ! Her magic flow'rs at once let's try.
                        (*gives each a white and red rose*)
    They'll serve but once, the leaves plucked from each
        stem
    For my relief, there's no re-leaving them.

        Glee.—Air, " When the wind blows."

            When the wind blows
            Strip from the rose,
        A leaf so light and airy ;

> Where the leaf drops
> There we all stops,
> So I think we'll obey the fairy.

Air, " The whole Hog or none."

PRINCE. So come let's on, nor care about what dangers
    we may run.
SPOON. Right! now we're in for it, let's go the whole hog
    or none.
    I'd bet a trifle we succeed.
PRINCE.   To that I'd too say " done."
    Nay, I'd stake my whole existence——
ALL.   Good! the whole hog or none.
    Oh, lawks, girls! I'll bet you any money,
    We'll find the one we want, or if we don't, it's funny.
    Since to seek her, we'll just go the whole hog or none.
    (*repeat*) Oh, lawks, girls, &c.   *Dance off,* L. 1 E.

SCENE SECOND.—*The Borders of the Golden Land.*

Enter TURKO, *surnamed the Terrible, followed by* MEELI-
MUG *and* OFFICERS, R.

TURK. Bid our troops halt.
MEELI.   Halt!
OFFICERS. (*outside*)   Halt!
MEELI.   'Tis done, great king.
TURK. So; let the foremost rank stand at the wing.
    An old stage trick—the audience by those means
    May think we've hundreds more behind the scenes.
    Thus far we've marched without impediment,
    On rapine, pillage, and destruction bent.
MEELI. Your gracious majesty ——
TURK.   Peace, slave, audacious—
    How dare you say my majesty is gracious?
    To such a character I'm no aspirant—
    I'm proud to say that I'm a reg'lar tyrant.
MEELI. Pardon, great king—but may we ask the reason
    Why this our peaceful neighbour's lands we seize on?
    King Buonacore has not harmed us——

TURK.   Stuff!
MEELI. What is our cause of quarrel?
TURK.   He's a muff!
   I hate him and his notions, weak and sappy—
   A king to try and make his subjects happy!
   Beneath his reign no sorrow, no complaining—
   Where all is sunshine—you can't call it *reigning*.
   No ruler he who thus to all men truckles,
   Give me a ruler that will rap folks' knuckles—
   Make them all wretched—that's the way I rule,
   A reg'lar tyrant of the good old school.

Song.— Air, " The Fine Old English Gentleman."

I'll sing a good old song of the monarch truly great,
The fine old-fashioned tyrant of the school legitimate.
Who scorns the namby pamby rule of kings effeminate;
And much above his subjects' love, prefers his people's
    hate.
   Like a fine old-fashioned tyrant, one of the olden style.

Beneath my sway I'm proud to say no joy is ever known,
No smile e'er seen, except upon our royal lips alone.
Each living thing, except the king, must weep and sigh
    and groan,
Which makes it all the pleasanter to occupy the throne.
   Like a fine old-fashioned tyrant, one of the olden style.

But times are changing rapidly, kings now their thoughts
    employ
On constitutions, letting folks their liberty enjoy;
Retrenchment, peace, reform, they cry; such trash shan't
    me annoy.
I'll tyrannise, I'll trample down, burn, pillage, and destroy.
   Like a fine old-fashioned tyrant, one of the olden style.

   Ha! Gruffangrimio comes—his aspect sinister
   Shows a prime fellow—not alone prime minister.

Enter GRUFFANGRIMIO, R.

   My friend——.
GRUFF. (R.)   My liege——
TURK. (L.)   Our business to begin,
   There is a matter you can serve me in.

GRUFF. That I can serve you *in?* (*aside*) Ha, ha! no doubt,
   The day will come when I may serve you out.
TURK. Listen! (*three green leaves fly rapidly in,* L, *and*
        hit him in the face) What's that? My eye!
        (*rubbing it*) Say, what are those leaves?
MEEL. (L., *picking them up*) Your Majesty, they look to
   me like rose leaves :
TURK. (C.) Confound their rosy cheek! there's malice
   seen in it;
   They'd have our royal eye with something green in it.
   Was such cool impudence e'er seen?
GRUFF. (R.)   Who knows?
   I ne'er saw anything *couleur de rose;*
   Of most things, I take gloomy views at best,
   And don't particularly like the rest.
TURK. (*looking off*) See, who comes here?

Enter PRINCE, COUNTS MUFFIO *and* SPOONIO *hastily,* L.

PRINCE. (C.)   Good sirs, excuse me, pray,
   But have you seen three rose leaves pass this way?
   I had them in my eye but now. They've flown——
TURK. (R. C.) Your eye? 'Tis false; I had them in my own.
   Guards, seize those traitors—hang up all the lot!
        (GUARDS *put ropes round their necks*)
   Those leaves had blinded me as lief as not;
   Upon the topmost branches hung—good reason,
   Their crime and punishment alike—*high trees on.*

Concerted Music. Air, " The Beggar Girl."

PRINCE. Pity, good gentlemen, show some humanity,
   Cold blows the wind on folks hung out to dry.
SPOON. Give us not cause, sir, to question your sanity,
   'Twas your own fault for not minding your eye.
TURKO. String 'em up, swing 'em up—wounding my vanity,
   Now they add insult unto injury.
MUFF. Pity, good gentlemen, bind us by any tie,
   To you in gratitude—never say " die."
       (PRINCE, MUFFIO, *and* SPOONIO *repeat in chorus*)
   Pity, good gentlemen, show some humanity,
   'Twas your own fault for not minding your eye.

TURKO. Hold! (*signs to* GUARDS *who release them*) A
        bright thought has in my brain to dwell come.
GRUFF. Then, pray you, as a stranger, give it welcome.
TURKO. I have at home three daughters all unmarried,
    These pris'ners to my palace shall be carried ;
    There should they fall in love, as I expect,
    Each shall her husband—each his bride select.
PRINCE. Hold, crafty tyrant! you o'errate your pow'r,
    Your craft won't do three nuptial knots an hour,
    One maid alone will I e'er marry.
TURKO.   True—
    He'd be a bold man who would marry two !
GRUFF. (*disgusted*) You mean to make them happy ?
TURKO.   No, I don't,
    That's not my will—you know it's not my *wont ;*
    Make half a dozen people happy thus,
    No ; that half dozen *doesn' half* suit us.
    (*taking him aside*) If one the youngest for his bride
        would take,
    We'll him the husband of the eldest make ;
    Whichever each *don't* choose, that one he *shall* have,
    So each young fellow will the other's gal have ;
    Thus to all six you see we misery bring.
    D'ye like the plan ?
GRUFF.   I don't like anything ;
    But a day will come——
TURK.   Eh ?
GRUFF. (*starting from a reverie*) I didn't speak.
TURK. What day will come ?
GRUFF. (*confused*) Well, say next Monday week.
MUFF. (*to* PRINCE) Against our peace they're plotting.
PRINCE.   Well, fear not.
    No piece is any good without a plot.
    Can't you take a leaf out of my book, eh ?
SPOON. We did take a leaf out of your bouquet,
    Which here conducted us.
PRINCE.   Peace, coward, elves,
    And learn in future to conduct yourselves.
MUFF. Let's smell the roses, and escape——
PRINCE.   No need to,
    Until we see what this adventure 'll lead to.
    We can do that at any time.

TURK. (c.)   Halloa!
  What's all this whispering?
GRUFF. (*aside*, R.)   Why don't they go.
  O'ercharged with bile, find vent in speech I must,
  Or, like an o'ercharged biler, I shall bust.
TURK. Come; here's of misery such a prospect pleasant,
  Our warlike notions we'll forego at present.
  Home again! march! guards, to your prisoners see.
          Music.—Exeunt all but GRUFFANGRIMIO, R.
GRUFF. They're gone! and now for my soliloquy.
                          (*pacing stage*)
  Tremble! Revenge!—Ha, ha! He's out of hearing,
  And I my plots may speak of without fearing.
  Tremble, proud tyrant! Here I vengeance vow
  It shall o'ertake thee—though I don't know how;
  A day of reckoning is at hand! Till then
  My vengeance sleeps—though I can't say till when;
  But I'll a deed perform,—although I've not
  At present the remotest notion what—
  Which in the dust shall lay your pride so high,
  Tremble then, tyrant—though I don't know why.—
  What, then? 'Tis not for men like me to care for
  The how, the when, the what, the why, the wherefore.

  Song.—Air, "Ridin' in a Railroad Car."

On terrible thoughts of vengeance bent,
    Strange plots and projects are,
Rushing through my pate at as quick a rate
    As if ridin' in a railroad car.
A day will come, I swear by gum,
    Of reckoning, when—ha! ha!
I rush on the foe as swift as though
    A ridin' in a railroad car.
King Turko's crown in the dust dragged down,
    I'll start for realms afar;
Whence another king I'll hither bring,
    A ridin' in triumphal car.
Then comes general crash, universal smash,
    A breaking up regular;
Like the smash we get when by chance upset,
    A ridin' in a railroad car.   *Dances off*, R.

Scene Third.—*Gardens of the Palace of King Turko.*

PAS MAURESQUE.

BY THE LADIES OF THE COURT.

Enter Tartarella, R. U. E.

Tartar. There, that will do; of course you mice will play,
    The moment that the royal cat's away.
    Your gladness vexes me—be off! get out!

Exeunt Dancers.

    My father's absence is a treat no doubt;
    Since he's been gone the court's one scene of jollity,
    Regardless of age, sex, condition, quality—
    Grave duchesses with skipping ropes are seen;
    While noble lords play leap-frog on the green.

    Song—Tartarella—*Air from* "*Norma.*"

    Now papa has gone—their joy thus marking,
    The court itself gives up to larking.

    Air changes to—"*Far, Far upon the Sea.*"

    Far, far and wide we see
    All their lordships on the spree,
   Their highnesses, their graces, young and old,
    Going in for mirth and fun,
    As if every mother's son
  Of himself to make a fool, the Fates had told.
    Each one hops, or skips, or jumps,
    Or at cricket stirs his stumps,
  Some at rounders, pitch and toss, or tipcat play;
    Or they're shooting in the ring,
    Flying kites, or anything.
Oh, gaily sport the mice when the cat's away.
      Far, far from home is he,
      His ungracious majesty,
    To return, we trust, not yet for many a day,
      In his presence all were sad,
      In his absence all gone mad,
    So gaily sport the mice when the cat's away.

    Enter Dragonetta, *bowling a hoop*, L. U. E.

Drag. Out of the way there—mind the hoop, don't stop it.
    There now, you spiteful thing—you've made me drop it.

TART. (L.) Sister, you bowling hoops! Oh, fie! for shame.
DRAG. (R.) Why blame my sport, pray—what's your
  little game?
  Now pa has left us, like the rest I try,
  But can't enjoy myself, I don't know why.
  I play at ball—soon tire the ball of flinging.
  I'm sick of skipping—still more sick with swinging.
  I bowl my hoop, then as the hoop runs off,
  I lose my breath and get a *hooping* cough.
  P'raps I've outgrown this romping harum scarum.
  Girls should cease bowling hoops, when once they
    wear 'em.
TART. The court has all gone mad I think.
DRAG.   No wonder,
  By that old cross-patch of a king kept under;
  Caused by his temper, of all joys the loss;
  Like Northern trains, all starting from *King's Cross.*
TART. 'Tis true while here all mirth he firmly checked.
DRAG. The brute! of course I speak with all respect.
TART. Nay, sister, pray.
DRAG.   You love him, don't you? Stuff.
TART. My duty as a daughter——
DRAG.   That's enough.
  His absence is a boon, naught could be more clearer.
  Were he no father, you'd not have him nearer.
  Nobody cares for him.

Enter VIOLET, R.

VIOLET. (C.)   You're wrong. I do.
DRAG. (R.) You care for him, child!—pooh! Who cares
  for you.
VIOLET. Shame on you, sisters! Faults let others find.
  To parents' failings children should be blind.
  What if he is harsh, stern, and all the rest of it;
  Things might be worse—smile, then, and make the
    best of it.
TART. (L.) His cruelties don't strike you p'raps as such.
VIOLET. Strike me? oh, don't they; but they don't hurt
  much.
DRAG. His tyranny beats everything.
TART.   That's true.

VIOLET. Why grumble then if it sometimes beats you?
DRAG. For a whole day he'll give us nought to eat.
VIOLET. Making next morning's breakfast quite a treat.
TART. No happiness he suffers in this place.
VIOLET. What? when we gaze on nature's smiling face.
  Hear the glad song of birds—there's one now, hark!
  Singing up yonder—what a jolly lark!
  Joys such as these to stop's a task above him.
DRAG. Can you defend him?
VIOLET.   No, but I can love him.
DRAG. The girl's an idiot.
TART.   To dare presume
  To lecture us. Go, child, to your own room.
VIOLET. My room; but why?
DRAG.   Because your room would be
  Much more agreeable than your company.
TART. Go, child; don't vex us or you'll find us rather
  Inclined in temper to take after father.
VIOLET. Nay, sisters dear——
TART.   Go, or your face we'll smack.
  You're much too forward, you want taking back.
VIOLET. My ears are tingling, your harsh language shocks
    them.
DRAG. They'll tingle more if you don't go—I'll box them.

Concerted Music (Martha).

DRAG. & TART.   To your room, miss,
       Don't presume, miss,
        To lecture thus,
        And talk to us;
        Your elders we,
       And you shall see
      Your betters every way.

VIOLET.   You may beat me
       And ill treat me
        How e'er you will,
        My father still
        I'll love, respect,
       Nor recollect
      His faults whate'er you say.

          (change of music)

VIOLET.   No child should a parent's
              Faults too closely criticize,
            What of good apparent's
              In his character let's prize.
DRAG. & TART. Go, child! could a parent's
              Claims cause us to shut our eyes.
            Your talk would a parent's
              Influence quite neutralize.

ensemble.

              (*they drive* VIOLET *off* R.)

TART. A forward minx!   She stuck up for the king
    As if——
DRAG.   She always was a stuck up thing
TART. But see! methinks I see my father! (*looks off*)
DRAG.   Where?
    Come back already?—too bad, I declare!

        Enter TURKO, *dragging in an* OLD LORD, L.

LORD. Oh, spare me!
TURK.   Slave, I caught you on the hop.
DRAG. Caught! what about?
TURK. (L. C.)   About to spin a top.
    With string in hand I caught him in the act,
    The winding-up act we may say in fact;
    All pleasure's 'gainst our laws—those laws he'd
        spurn 'em,
    And topsy-turvey with his tops he'd turn 'em.
    Away with him! (*to* DAUGHTERS) Have you been
        happy, pray?
DRAG. Who could be happy, sir, when you're away?
TART. None in their monarch's absence— don't suppose it;
TURK. Nor in his presence if their monarch knows it.
    But come, I've brought you home a husband each,
TART. A husband!
DRAG.   Spare our blushes I beseech.
TURK. Bring in the pris'ners!

        PRINCE, MUFFIO, *and* SPOONIO *brought in* L.

                    There, your time don't lose,
    In blushing; but let each her husband choose.

MUFF. (*aside*) Magnificent! what dignity! what grace!
(*admiring* TARTARELLA)

SPOON. Your Highness, there's a figure—there's a face!
(*admiring* DRAGONETTA)

　　Such as you'd find in some romance's pages;

PRINCE. (c.) Yes; the romances of the middle ages.
　　The woman's forty if she is a day;

SPOON. Softly, piano with that *forte* pray.

TURK. Come, girls, your choice!

DRAG. (R. C.)　　　　　　If maiden diffidence
　　Would let me——

TURK.　　　　　Maiden fiddlesticks! commence.

DRAG. Here, then, I choose—— (*taking* PRINCE'S *hand*)

TARTAR.　　　　　· No—that you don't, indeed;
　　I'd fixed on him——

TURK.　　　　　Good! now, my plans succeed:

DRAG. I spoke first——

TARTAR.　　　　You shan't have him;

DRAG.　　　　　　　Shan't I, neither?

TURK. No: since both want him, he shan't marry either.

PRINCE. Thanks, king! Than wed with either, I make oath
　　I'd sooner die;

TURK.　　　　　Then you shall marry both.

PRINCE. Marry them both? Myself I think I see;
　　What! little me! No; 'twould be *bigamy*.

TURK. Peace—we will hear your friends' decision first;
　　Speak, sirs;

SPOON.　　　　If for such bliss, to hope, I durst,
　　This lovely maid—— (*approaching* DRAGONETTA)

DRAG.　　　　　Dear sensible young man!

SPOON. Say, could you love me?

DRAG.　　　　　　　To be sure I can;
　　As for that other—who a thought would waste
　　On one so utterly devoid of taste?

MUFF. And you, sweet creature, dare I ask could you——
(*to* TARTARELLA)

TARTAR. I know exactly what you mean—I do. (*giving hand*)

TURK. You shall be married instantly.

DRAG.　　　　　　　Oh, bliss!

TURK. Just so; but you take this one—and you this.

(separates the two couples and reverses them, giving
        SPOONIO *to* TARTARELLA, MUFFIO *to* DRAGONETTA)
DRAG. Oh, no !
TURK.   Delightful! finest of all sells,
    Ringing the changes on their marriage belles.
DRAG. Spare us this misery——
TURK.   No—this, I jolly call ;
    First-rate—stupendous—downright diabolical.

        (DRAGONETTA, TARTARELLA, SPOONIO *and* MUFFIO
            retire up)

        (*to* PRINCE) What we can do for you, I know not.
PRINCE.   See !
    There's one who has already done for me ;

                Enter VIOLET, R.

    The idol of my dreams, sweet maid.
VIOLET.   Oh dear !
    What's come to me ? I feel so funny here—
                    (*laying her hand on her heart*)
    Just in my heart a something seemed to strike it.
PRINCE. And did it hurt you ?
VIOLET.   No—I think I like it.
PRINCE. Dear maid, long loved, long sought, now found !
VIOLET.   What mean you ?
    Explain—until this moment I've ne'er seen you.
PRINCE. Yet often, in the land of dreams I've met you—
    Where Morpheus reigns——
VIOLET.   No wonder I forget you.
    Folks *met in Morpheus'* land one scarce can know,
    That *metamorphosis* does change them so.
    And you've been seeking for me ?
PRINCE.   Far and wide.
    In each point of the compass I have tried
    One point to compass—you to make my bride.
    North, southward, eastward, I have sought for you,
    Then I've gone to *sequestered* places, too.
    Deep glade, cool grot and mossy cell—my motto—
    Forget no cave—remember, please, the grotto.
VIOLET. All this to win my love ?—reflection sweet—
    My little hand the prize of your great feat.

Brave boy of miles for my sake walked—oh, joy—
My own brave Walker! my own Miles's boy.
PRINCE. Oh, happiness! she loves me then!
TURK. (c., *aside*)   So, so!
I think I've giv'n them rope enough. (*aloud*) Halloa!
VIOLET. (R.) Yes, pa.
PRINCE. (R. C.)   Your Majesty.
TURK.   Attend to me—
Are you in love yet?
PRINCE.   Deep as deep could be.
VIOLET. Yes, pa, indeed.
PRINCE.   At once to me pray give her.
TURK. Capital! chuck that fellow in the river—
The rest see married as I've settled.
VIOLET.   Nay,
Spare him!
TART.   Spare me!
DRAG.   Spare all of us!
TURK.   Away!

Concerted Music.—Air, " Ah, che la Morte." (*Trovatore*)

PRINCE. Ah! can a mortal glory,
    In such a sell severe?
    Think not that we, sir, feel fear—
    Oh dear, no, we but despise your pow'r 'tis clear.
VIOLET. Your children before ye,
    For pity implore ye;
    This misery spare us, pa, oh do like a dear.
    So all will adore ye—
    So please good papa, kind papa,
    Dear papa, to our pleading give ear.
    Do pray, yes say.
TURK.   No!

Air, " Sally come up."

For 'tis, shall I keep up, or shall I lay down,
My chief ambition and renown—
A tyrant be from toe to crown;
    So stern none me shall diddle.
Oh 'tis a sell, I like it well,
The four be wed, and drown'd instead,
    The other indiwiddle.

(two tunes harmonised)

OMNES. Oh, 'tis a sell, to hope farewell.
We've woe found instead
Of the wheel of fortune here.

VIOLET. Oh, no! Oh, no! spare him, pa,
Spare him! Cut not hope's
Thread thus in the middle.

PRINCE. Ah! can a mortal glory
Life's thread to cut thus in the middle?

TURK. Four tied up and one tied down
Fast in a sack. They're all done brown.
The river flows close beside the town,
That fellow chuck in the middle.

———

TURK. Seize them, guards!

PRINCE. *(giving words of command,* R. C.) Halt! attention!
So,! that's well.
Draw roses! present noses! ready! smell!
*(Chord—*SPOONIO *and* MUFFIO *obey, and at once
become invisible)*

TURK. (L.) What's this? those flowers—those youths both
gone—Forsooth!
Cut off——

PRINCE. (R. C.) Each in the flower of his youth.
Each smelt a rose, its magic scent——

TURK. True, true,
Its magic scent; but where's it sent 'em to?

DRAG. (C.) Gone!

TART. (R) Gone!

VIOLET. (R. C.) How gone! they still are standing there.

TURK. Sweet child, inform your loving father where.

PRINCE. You see them?

VIOLET. Both quite plain.

DRAG. Both, slanderer vain?
My lovely youth, none ever saw *him* plain.

PRINCE. What does this mean?

VIOLET. I wear around my neck
This charm which all enchantment holds in check.

TURK. Lend it to me.

VIOLET. I can't.

TURK. Point out the spot
Where they are standing then.

VIOLET. For worlds I'd not.

TURK. She sees 'em and we can't; be foiled I won't.
    Guards, seize 'em if you sees 'em.
OFFICER.   But we don't.
SPOON. Fear not, dear maid (*to* DRAGONETTA). My voice I
    can't make heard.
MUFF. Sweetest, I'm here (*to* TARTARELLA). She doesn't
    hear a word.
TART. I feel an arm about my waist, what's this?
                           (MUFFIO *embracing her*)
DRAG. Good gracious! I could swear I felt a kiss.
                          (SPOONIO *kissing her*)
VIOLET. Sisters, for shame; here in a public place,
    To let your lovers kiss you and embrace.
DRAG. 'Tis false—we didn't.
TURK.   What! they're there you say.
    Upon them guards! (MUFFIO *and* SPOONIO *retire up*)
VIOLET.   Nay, now they've gone away.
TURK. Seize somebody! do something! I don't care
    Who—what it is. Stay, seize that fellow there.
PRINCE. This fellow! Try it! Like the rest, he'll be
    Invisible—no more a *fellow de see,*
    Though with himself he makes away. Behold!
    (*about to smell the rose,* TURKO *snatches it from him*)
TURK. Ha! ha!
PRINCE.   My magic rose! lost, swindled, sold!

    PRINCE *and* VIOLET *embrace*—TURKO *and* GUARDS
    drag them apart, and ultimately force PRINCE
    off, L., *leaving* VIOLET *alone upon the scene; she*
    looks after them despairingly.

Scena.—VIOLET.—" *Tacea la notte*" (*Trovatore*).

Despair! oh fortune wretched, ah!
    I weep and sigh in vain, oh!
My love thus from me snatchèd ah!
    I ne'er shall see again, oh!
He'll not escape from pa, no!
No hope is left him, ah—no!

    Weep, wretched maiden, weep away.
    Yet stay, yet stay.
Some fairy power I know, will save him yet and so,
    Oh joy! let's all be gay!

"*Cabaletta.*"

New hopes within me growing;
My heart's with joy o'erflowing,
Although I'm far from knowing
What are those hopes, or why, or whence they spring.
    What then, when hearts are aching,
    Indeed we may say breaking,
    If hope comes all right making—
To ask that hope's address is not the thing—
    No, no, no, no!
But hope's come somehow, so with joy—I sing.

Exit, R.

Enter FAIRY, R. U. E.

FAIRY. My protégés in trouble—I, who gave them
That talisman—those roses—yet will save them;
Ho! fairies, this way flock from each direction,
And take these lovers under your protection.
    (*beckons on* FAIRIES *from various entrances*)

MOUVEMENT DES FEES.

(*Tableau closed in by*

SCENE FOURTH.—*Corridor of the Palace, leading to the
Prince's Dungeon.*

Enter GRUFFANGRIMIO, R., *with a large bunch of keys, a
rope, and an empty sack.*

GRUFF. One bird we've caged, though two have flown away;
    One bird in hand's worth two i' th' bush, they say.
    The tyrant Turko, whom I serve (of course,
    Only till I my scheme can put in force;
    Which had been long since were I not prevented
    By one fact—that my scheme's not yet invented.)
    The tyrant Turko—once more to go back—
    Whom I still serve, though I have got the sack;
                      (*producing it*)
    Bids me, the prisoner, with this bag to kiver,
    Then bag and baggage chuck him in the river.
    Now for it! So, the bag's all right, I guess;
    As for the baggage— (*looking off*) Ha! the young
        Princess!

c

Enter VIOLET, L.

VIOLET. My lord!

GRUFF.   My lady!

VIOLET.   How shall I begin:
  Is the young Prince, your prisoner, within?

GRUFF. In deepest dungeon chained—he's in no doubt,
  In fact he's so deep you'd ne'er find him out.

VIOLET. Good! I would speak with him.

GRUFF.   No, would you really.

VIOLET. You'll not refuse——

GRUFF.   You love him, then?

VIOLET.   Yes, dearly.
  Come, take this silken purse filled full of gold.

GRUFF. Pshaw! I make more by doing as I'm told—
  Here in the river souse him.

VIOLET.   Hold! No fear!
  You'll make no silk purse out of that *souse here ;*
  You drown my love! attempt it and you'll rue it.

GRUFF. Well, wait a minute, you shall see me do it.
  Goes to door, R., *and commences unfastening bolts, &c.*

VIOLET. (*calling,* L.) Come, lords, your friend to save
          quick, hasten hither!

Enter MUFFIO *and* SPOONIO *hastily,* L.

GRUFF. (*turning abruptly*) Who's there? By Jove! I
          thought she'd some one with her.

VIOLET. Upon him, friends—fear not—he cannot see you.
          (*the two* LORDS *attack* GRUFFANGRIMIO, *knocking down,*
          and holding him there)

GRUFF. Who and what's this?

VIOLET.   And now, dear Prince, to free you.
          Unfastens door, and exit into prison, R.

GRUFF. (C.) There's no one here—yet something knocked
          me down,
  Could that be spirit-rapping cracked my crown—
  Held down too! who's there?

MUFF. (L. *shouting*)   Villain!

GRUFF.   No reply!
          Who's there?

SPOON. (R.) Knave! he can't hear me, by-the-bye.

Re-enter VIOLET, *leading in* PRINCE, R.

VIOLET. Dear Prince, you're free.

GRUFF.   Help, guards!

VIOLET.   Quick! muzzle, gag him,
Bind him!

PRINCE.   And stay—in his own sack we'll bag him.
(*Music.— the four bind* GRUFFANGRIMIO *with ropes,
and put sack over him, he struggling*)
To my late dungeon drag the cut-throat grim,
It was my cell, 'twill be a sell for him.

Music. — " *The Cure*"—*they jump him off through door*, R.
And now, my love, my beautiful, my own,
One fond embrace!

VIOLET. (C.)   Nay, Prince, we're not alone.
Your friends, invisible to all but me,
Are present.

PRINCE. (L.)   Absent friends I'd have them be.
Bid them go home at once.

SPOON. (R.)   If I'm *de trop.*

VIOLET. He hears you not, but wishes you to go.
I, by this talisman hear and behold you.

PRINCE. Which *tallies, man,* with what before she told you.
Go home, friends; my adventures here make known;
Get out of my way and get on your own,
As pioneers before me go.   It's clear
We don't want you to stop a *spyin' here.*

MUFF. (L.) Spying! I scorn the charge, your Highness.

VIOLET.   Hence!
You can't be heard, e'en in your own defence.

SPOON. (L. C.) He shares the silent spell that's over-
come me,
My partner in this game of double dummy.

MUFF. I humbly take my leave.

VIOLET.   That's right—away!
Go, and don't talk about it.

SPOON.   I obey.

                    Exeunt MUFFIO *and* SPOONIO, L.

PRINCE. (L.) Well, have they gone?

VIOLET. (R.)   They have.

PRINCE.   Then in that case,
As I observed before, one fond embrace,

VIOLET. Dear Prince, will you be always true thus?
PRINCE.   How ?
VIOLET. I mean, dear, will you love me then as now?
PRINCE. Then! when?
VIOLET.   I don't know, but I thought I'd ask,
    P'raps it's when hollow hearts shall wear a mask.
    No matter when, you'll love me still.
PRINCE.   I swear
    To love you madly, madder than March hare,
    Yes, till all nature, earth, air, seas and skies,
    Each living thing that walks, crawls, swims or flies,
    Alike assumes of indigo the hue.
    In other words—I'll love till all is blue.

Duet.—Air, "Ama tua madre," Lucrezia Borgia.

PRINCE.   Thus I my fond troth plighting,
                Promise to make you mine, love;
           If you'd like it in writing,
                I will the paper sign, love.
           But when hearts are fond, love,
           Words are good as bond.
BOTH.   Yes, when hearts are fond, &c.

VIOLET.   Thus I your troth receiving,
             ͨ Oh what delight is mine, love,
           I your true faith believing,
                You need no paper sign, love.
           For when hearts are fond, love,
                Words are good as bond.
BOTH.   Yes, when hearts are fond, &c.

VIOLET. But hark!—a footstep! If you're found, you're
        lost !
    Your flight must be secured at any cost.
    So follow my advice, and—follow me.
PRINCE. In every sense your follower I'd be. *Exeunt,* R.

Enter DRAGONETTA, L.

Duet.—Air, " The Blue Bells of Scotland.

DRAG. Oh, where, and oh where is my own dear Spoonio
        gone ?

Enter TARTARELLA, L.

TARTAR. (*singing*) Oh where, and oh where is my lovely
    Muffio gone ?
DRAG. They have gone on some strange scent.
TARTAR.   Without our assent they're flown.
BOTH. And it's—oh ! in our hearts that we wish they hadn't
    gone.

TARTAR. What horrid spell—in scent of roses pent?
DRAG. Spells should be harmless when they're in-a-scent.
TARTAR. Heigho ! to think the perfume of a flow'r
    To carry off two men should have the pow'r.
DRAG. Those roses' perfume was indeed a strong scent.
TARTAR. The scent they've gone on seems for us the
    wrong scent.
DRAG. Heigho !

Enter SPOONIO, L.

SPOON.   Myself away I cannot tear—
    Without once more beholding her.
                   (*embracing* DRAGONETTA)
DRAG.   Who's there ?
    Is it my Spoonio come back to cheer me ?
SPOON. Yes, dear, 'tis I—alas, she cannot hear me.

  Duet.—Air, " *It is a charming girl I love.*"—*Lily of*
    Killarney.

SPOON.   It is this charming girl I love,
        Yet know not how to woo her ;
    I'd say she's prized all maids above,
        She'd hear no word said to her.
    Her eyes are piercers, 'tis most true,
    They literally me look through.
    I call to her, with cries forlorn,
    But not to her's my calling borne.

DRAG.   Botheration ! botheration !
        My lover I can't hear or see.
SPOON.   There is but one girl I love,
        And she cannot see me.
DRAG. (*repeat*) Botheration, &c.

TART. How, sister, are you mad ?

Enter MUFFIO, L.

MUFF.   I cannot go
Without one kiss ere leaving her. (*kisses* TARTARELLA)
TART.   Halloa !
'Tis he—my Muffio—speak !
MUFF.   You're right, 'tis I.
DRAG. (R.) Speak to me, Spoonio.
TART. (L. C.)   Muffio, dear, reply.
DRAG. Show yourself, Spoonio, if you love me do.
TART. Dear Muffio, let me see you—if it's you.
SPOON. (R. C., *taking out red rose*) To smell or not to
          smell, that is the question.
Whether obey stern prudence's suggestion,
Or to take heart against this sea of woes,
And by one sniff to end 'em—yes—here goes.
DRAG. Dear gentlemen——
SPOON.   All caution hence I'll pitch—
I'll be a gentleman, and act as sich. (*smells the rose*)
DRAG. (*embracing him*) 'Tis he—oh, joy !
MUFF.   So—so—I see the game,
He's smelt the red rose.   Good—I'll do the same.
                                    (*smells it*)
TART. (*embracing him*) 'Tis he !

Enter MEELIMUG *and* GUARDS, L.

MEELI.   Hold—eh! Just so—and hold 'em fast ;
So then, the runaways we've caught at last ;
To prison with all four !
DRAG.   Touch us who dares !
MEELI. We've to arrest you—you two loving pairs.
DRAG. Knave, in your teeth I hurl the falsehood black,
That base-meant story of the two pair back.
MEELI. Away with them——
MUFF.   Why did I smell the rose ?
SPOON. They'll make us pay for smelling—through the nose.

Concerted Music.—Air, " Toll the Bell."

SPOON. Invisible still keeping, I in safety now might be,
DRAG. Forgive me, dear, 'twas my fault—I so wished your
          face to see ;

Muff. The white rose and the red one used—no other
    spell we've got;
Tart. All our hearts filled with sorrow—they've sold
    us all the lot.
(*all four*) Sold, sold again—a reg'lar cruel sell,
    No hope is left—that we know too well;
    We are swindled, done outright,
    We are circumvented quite;
      From the scrape no escape—
      Sold, sold again!
                 They are led off into prison, R.

Scene Fifth.—*Throne Room in King Turko's Palace.*

Enter Turko *with the magic rose,* R.

Turk. A glorious scheme I've in my brain just hatched;
    This magic rose I from my pris'ner snatched,
    Makes him invisible who smells it. Right!
    I'll try it on myself—so, out of sight,
    I can see all that passes in this place—
    What's said behind my back hear to my face.
    Seen by *no mortal eye,* their minds they'll speak;
    To flatter me *no more to lie* they'll seek.
    Thus I some wholesome truths shall hear, no doubt;
    And let the chaps I hear them from look out.
    Who comes? My ministers? So——   (*smells rose*)

Enter Gruffangrimio *and* Meelimug, *cautiously,* L.

Gruff.   Not a word,
    Until we're certain we're not overheard.
                  (*they look round the room*)
Meeli. (R.) All's secure! We're *alone!*
Turk. (C., *aside*)   Though you may be
    A *loan,* I question the security.
Gruff. (L.) Listen! the king, whose hated rule we suffer,
    A compound of the fool—the knave—the duffer;
    Old, ugly, silly, cowardly, and spiteful.
Meeli. His portrait to the life!
Turk. (*aside*)   This is delightful!
Gruff. Not long we'll bow our heads to him as now.
Turk. (*aside*) True; for you'll shortly have no heads to
      bow.

MEELI. What are your plans to change this harsh monotony?
GRUFF. I grieve to say as yet I haven't got any;
    But time will come—till then we must dissemble.
TURK. I think I've heard enough. (*shouting*) Ho, villains,
        tremble!
GRUFF. Yes, land oppressed, we'll of this tyrant rid you.
TURK. Villains! why don't you tremble when I bid you.
    They hear me not—thanks to that rose I smelt;
    Unseen, unheard, I'll make my presence felt.
                    (*kicks* MEELIMUG *violently*)
MEELI. Oh, murder!
GRUFF.   What?
MEELI.   Somebody or something
    Kicked me just now.
GRUFF.   Stay, should it be the king.
                   (TURKO *kicks him*)
    It is! the matter past all doubt is put.
    Too well I recognise the royal foot.
    Spare us, your majesty. (*falling on his knees*)
MEELI. (*kneeling*) Great king!
TURK. (*calling*)   What ho!
    Guards, seize these traitors! No reply.
GRUFF. (*looking round*)   Halloa!
    None here.
MEELI.   Some bootless idle fancy tricked us.
GRUFF. No 'twasn't bootless whatsoever kicked us.

          Enter an OFFICER, L.

OFFICER. King Buonocore at the palace gate
    Requests admission.
TURK.   Bid the fellow wait;
    We're busy.
GRUFF.   Show him in at once.
TURK.   Hey dey!
    Our orders questioned! Show him out I say.
GRUFF. Stay, where's King Turko?
TURK. (*very loud*)   Here! (*standing between them*)
OFFICER.   ·   He can't be found;
    We've searched for him in vain the palace round.
GRUFF. Good!   *Exit* OFFICER, L.

(TURKO *crosses to* R. C., *between* MEELIMUG *and*
      GRUFFANGRIMIO)
            This king's presence here, suggests a plot;
We'll get up a rebellion on the spot—
Vacant declare the throne.
TURK.   Not if I know it. (*goes and sits on throne*)
GRUFF. And upon Buonocore we'll bestow it.
MEEL. Declare the throne a vacancy.
GRUFF.   No less!
      Thus we a *vay can see* to our success.
OFFICER. (*announcing*) King Buonocore and the Lord
      Kootoo!

      Enter BUONOCORE *and* KOOTOO, L.

GRUFF. (R.C.) We're glad to see you both sirs, how d'ye do?
BUON. (L. C.) We'd see King Turko——
GRUFF.   Don't. Take my advice;
      His is a face you'd not wish to see twice.
TURK. (C.) Slaves! you shall pay for this;
GRUFF.   The tyrant's fled;
      Say sire, will you not be our king instead?   .
BUON. My luckless son I seek.
GRUFF.   Nay, think upon
      Your lucky stars, not your unlucky son;
      A throne awaiting you—who'd stand debating,
      See this chance thrown away, and throne awaiting?
BUON. Sir, such a thing's far from my thoughts.
GRUFF.   Pooh! pooh!
      Don't talk of far-things—here's a crown for you;
      Our people groan beneath this tyrant's curse,
      Groan worse each day—as he's each day grown worse.
TURK. (*screaming in a rage*) 'Tis false! slaves! traitors!
            How my rage to vent!
GRUFF. All's silent—does that silence give consent?
BUON. Well, yes!
GRUFF. ⎫
MEELI. ⎬   Long live King Buonocore!
KOOT. ⎭
BUON. ˙   So,
      I occupy this throne now vacant. (*sits on* TURKO'S *lap*)
TURK.   No!

(*Music.—He springs up and throws* BUONOCORE *off*)
BUON. Help! murder! speak! who and what are you? Say.

VIOLET *runs in*, R.

VIOLET. What noise is here? My father! hold, I pray;
Don't thus excite yourself, dear father.
GRUFF. (R.)   What?
He here?
BUON. (L. C.)   What father, child?—we see him not.
VIOLET. I recognize him, though, beneath a spell.
TURK. Wise child, who her own father knows so well.
GRUFF. Shall we obey a king who can't be seen?
To think so, he must be invisible green.
To a mere shadow king have deference paid—
No, we'll not be particular to a shade.
TURK. True, true—in every way I'm done. I've got
The what's-his-name to pay, and no pitch hot.
I choke! I stifle! madness! rage!
VIOLET. (*following him*)   Papa!
TURK. Don't talk to me! I'm raving mad! Ha, ha!
Exit furiously, R.—VIOLET *is following, when she
is met by*

PRINCE AMABEL *entering*, R.

PRINCE. Stay, dearest!
BUON.   Ah! 'tis he! my son, my boy!
PRINCE. Hah, gov'nor—see! I've found her—wish me joy.
BUON. I always do wish joy to every one.
GRUFF. (*aside*) How's this—his father—he! What have
I done?
Giv'n him a throne. Yet after all why not—
What matters it who reigns, so I can plot?
BUON. (*to* VIOLET) 'Twas you then stole his heart—'twas
felony.
VIOLET. 'Twas fell on two knees when he knelt to me.
PRINCE. Say to our union you consent.
BUON. (*joining their hands*)   I do.
VIOLET. Your pardon—till it's by *my* pa done, too.
PRINCE. What mean you?
VIOLET.   Press me not—be yours I can't
'Till my own father, too, his sanction grant.

KOOT. Come, sire, at once let's through the city go forth,
Proclaim you King, and see you crowned, and so forth.
VIOLET. What, 'gainst my father, then, revolt you raise?
GRUFF. Of course; we're sick of his revolting ways;
Besides, he's disappeared—on, friends—huzzah!
For revolution and a *coup d'etât*.

Exeunt all, L., but VIOLET *and the* PRINCE.

VIOLET. (R.) Hold! any *coup* but that——
PRINCE. (L.) Then if you're willing,
The cooing one associates with billing.
VIOLET. Say, do you love me, Prince?
PRINCE. Oh, don't I, rather.
VIOLET. Prove it by aiding me to save my father,
Act to him as a friend—thus shall we show pa—
He was in error when he proved a *foe pa*.
PRINCE. What can I do? Name but the boon, 'tis granted.
VIOLET. Thanks! By your kindness I'm like him enchanted.
PRINCE. Enchanted!
VIOLET. By that rose he took from you,
You have a countercharm will cure him.
PRINCE. True,
This last remaining rose will end his grief,
Prove his *last rose of summar*-y relief.
VIOLET. You'll give it him?
PRINCE. Yes, upon one condition,
That for our marriage he'll give his permission.
VIOLET. Nay, I'll have no conditions.
PRINCE. One alone,
My sole condition that you change your own.
VIOLET. If giv'n unconditional and free 'tis,
We'll make no bargains or commercial treaties;
We'll have no prices nor no tariffs.
PRINCE. Why?
Our tariff's not *tariff*ically high,
'Tis but our happiness secure to make.
VIOLET. And thus of him a mean advantage take.
No, save him first—then let him freely grant
Our prayer.
PRINCE. Should he refuse?
VIOLET. He won't—he can't.

Duet—Air, "My love is like the Red Red Rose."

PRINCE. Oh, my love would like this red red rose,
   Can I refuse the boon ?
VIOLET. But your love don't like this melody,
   Suppose we change the tune.

Air, "Giles Scroggins."

PRINCE. " Giles Scroggins," I instead propose.
VIOLET.   Right !
PRINCE.   Tol de riddle ol de ray !
   So my love would like this red red rose.
VIOLET.   Right !
PRINCE.   Tol de riddle ol de ray !

   About it pray make no ado, (*giving rose*)
   For if you loves I, as I love you,
   No strife must come between us two.
BOTH.   Ri tol de riddle ol de ray !

VIOLET. Thus yielding, you your love's truth prove.
PRINCE.   Right !
VIOLET.   Tol de riddle ol de ray !
   And every ling'ring doubt remove.
PRINCE.   Right !
VIOLET.   Tol de riddle ol de ray !
   So with affection fond and true,
   If you love's me as I love you,
   No knife shall cut our loves in two.
BOTH.   Ri tol de riddle ol de ray !   *Exeunt.* R.

SCENE SIXTH.—*A Public Place near the Capital.   Shouting
outside.*

Enter DRAGONETTA, TARTARELLA, SPOONIO *and* MUFFIO, L.

DRAG. That's right, my friends—shout, dance, and sing
   your best,
   From prison bars we've now a few bars rest.
   While there our song was one of dark despair,
   We've changed our tune, though, with this change
   of air.
TART. While there our only music seemed to be
   Locke's music—played with most discordant key.

MUFF. Prospects of hanging pointed but toward,
    What's called suspension of the common c(h)ord.
SPOON. While to make all of music emblematic,
    My prison room itself was upper-attic.
DRAG. Enough, my friends, our troubles now have ceased,
    Our new king has all prisoners released;
    Brought gladness to poor folks of hope bereft,
    All wrong's made right, while all that's right is left.
TART. The laws all changed too, in King Turko's time,
    To smile was treason, to be glad a crime.
    Now quite a different code we pay respect to !
DRAG. 'Tis a Revised Code no one can object to.
SPOON. What's come of Turko ?
MUFF.   No one knows !
DRAG.   And there's
    A strong suspicion also no one cares.
SPOON. Think you he's gone for good?
DRAG.   For good! not he!
    Gone to the bad, he's much more like to be.
TART. No one regrets his loss ; on every hand,
    Good riddance is the cry throughout the land.
SPOON. Deep in each heart, joy does his absence bring ;
    Deep-hearted joys, through this *departed* king.
MUFF. His innate cruelty, made him so hated !
DRAG. That which you term innate's now *terminated.*
    His reign is over—
MUFF.   True, we're happy thus,
    His reign is over—but not over us.
DRAG. Come friends! Come Spoonio dear, at once let's start!
    Give me your hand !
SPOON.   My hand ! with all my heart.
DRAG. On to the palace, there we'll take our station,
    To see King Buonocore's coronation.
                    Music.—Exeunt R.

Enter KING TURKO, R., *meeting them, but passing through
the midst of them unseen.*

TURK. Unhappy Turko! Terrible no more!
    How am I changed from what I was before ;
    None see, none hear, none care for me. 'Tis strange
    I seemed too bad a sovereign to change.

King Buonocore's throne 's fixed firm and steady :
(*aside*) Till my conspiracy against *him's* ready.
MEELI. Let's pitch old Turko in the river !
BUON.   Stay,
Good folks, let's have no quarreling I pray ;
The crown I've taken I resign !
MEELI.   ⎞
OFFICER. ⎬   You can't !
GUARDS. ⎠
BUON. To my own kingdom I'll return.
GUARDS, &c.   You shan't !
KOOT. Nay, if his majesty prefers to go,
Let him ; his son still can be king you know.
ALL. Long live King Amabel ! (*put royal robes on* PRINCE)
GRUFF. (*aside*)   My projects thrive ;
Another king dethroned as I'm alive.
PRINCE. As my first act of sovereignty I banish —
The late King Turko.
MEELI.   Come, old fellow, vanish.
TURK. Dog !
PRINCE.   Silence ! as the second—for my queen
I choose his daughter !
DRAG.   Which, sire, do you mean !
VIOLET. Nay, prince, it cannot be, I grieve to say.
Though love and inclination point one way—
My duty points the other.   I will share
My father's exile.

Enter FAIRY, *behind,* L.

FAIRY. (C.)   Not so, princess, fair,
Turko is not your father !
VIOLET.   How ! explain—
My father not my father.
TURK.   Sold again.
FAIRY. Turko's a vile usurper, you're the daughter
Of the true king.   That king did Turko slaughter.
Usurped his throne when you were but a baby.
VIOLET. That's why I don't remember it then, maybe.
FAIRY. Just so, you were in long clothes, he, in short—
TURK. Hold ! I confess, I'm a right down bad sort.

Still to continue, so shall be my plan ;
" Say, am I right." (*defiantly*) " Or any other man."
Fairy.   Scruple not then to share this prince's throne,
Since in your father's right it is your own.
Long, happy be your reign.
Prince.   Thanks! best of friends,
Our length of reign though scarce on you depends.
A higher power than yours appeal we now to—
One which prince, king, nay, fairies' selves must
bow to.
(*to* Audience) Say you, our Fairy Roses shall succeed,
Couleur de Rose all will be then indeed.

Finale—Air, "*Io son ricco, tu sei bella.*" (*Elisir d'Amore*)

Prince.   Of our roses your leaves taking,
                 Oh let not those roses fade.
Violet.   But your smiles a sunshine making,
                 Them to blossom say you'll aid.
Turk.   All my faults forgive—remember,
                 There's no rose without a thorn.
Gruff.   He repents in the finale,
                 Such an action I would scorn.
Tart.   Say you're pleased, the future we
                 Shall thus rosy tinted see.
Spoon.   In good odour dwell content,
                 Once assured of your *as-scent.*

(*ensemble*) Of our roses your leaves taking,
                 Oh let not those roses fade.
              But your smiles a sunshine making,
                 Them to blossom say you'll aid.
              If your're pleased, the future we
                 Shall all rosy tinted see.
              In good odour dwell content,
                 If we've your assent.

Scene opens, and discovers the
" VISION OF THE FLOWERY FUTURE !"

Curtain.

Printed by Thomas Scott, Warwick Court, Holborn.

Lacy's Acting Edition of Plays, 6d. each—

Or in Volumes, [Old Debts , at 7s. each, Post free.

ALPHABETICAL LIST

OF FULL LENGTH AND OTHER

ALBUM CARTE DE VISITE

DRAMATIC PORTRAITS

PHOTOGRAPHED FROM LIFE,

BY MESSRS.

BASSANO,	ROBINSON (*Dublin*),
CLARKINGTON,	SILVY,
HEATH AND BEAU,	WALKER,
JAMES,	WALL,
KEITH (*Liverpool*),	WATKINS, HERBERT,
KING (*Bath*),	WATKINS, JOHN,
MAYALL,	AND
MAYER, BROTHERS,	WATKINS, CHARLES,

AND THE PARISIAN PHOTOGRAPHERS.

One Shilling and Six Pence each

OR

Three Shillings, beautifully coloured

}post free

ON SALE, BY

THOMAS HAILES LACY, 89, STRAND, LONDON, W. C.

Postage Stamps received in payment.

	PORTRAITS		PORTRAITS
ADAMS, Miss, portrait	1	BEDFORD, Mr. Paul, portraits	4
,, ,, as *Rifleman*	1	,, with TOOLE in the Stocks	1
ADDISON, Mr., as *Old Trusty*	2	,, with TOOLE, *Willow Copse*	2
,, ,, in *Dearest Mamma*	2	,, *Turkish Bath*	1
,, ,, *Peep o' Day*	1	BEETHOVEN portrait	1
ALBONI, Mdlle., portraits	6	BELART, Signor ,,	2
ANDERSON, Mr. J. R. ,,	3	BELL, Mr. Robert ,,	1
,, ,, *Ingomar*	1	BELLETTI, Signor ,,	2
ANSON, Mr., portrait	1	BELLEW, Rev. ,,	2
ARDEN, Miss ,,	2	BENEDICT, Mr. ,,	2
ARDITI, Signor ,,	2	BENNETT, Mr. Sterndale, portraits	2
,, ,, comic portrait	1	BEVERLEY, Mr. W. ,,	1
ATKINSON, Miss, portrait	1	BILLINGTON, Mr. ,,	2
,, ,, *Lady Macbeth*	1	BILLINGTON, Mrs. ,,	2
,, ,, *Lady Constance*	1	,, Mr. & Mrs., portrait	1
,, ,, *Winter's Tale*	1	BLAND, Miss Kate ,,	1
		BLONDIN	3
BACH, composer, portrait	1	,, (costume)	2
BALFE, Mr. ,,	2	,, Family (The)	1
BALFE, Miss ,,	1	BORGHI-MAMO, Madame, portrait	1
BALL, Mr. Lewis ,,	1	,, ,, in *Prophet*	2
BANKS, Miss ,,	1	,, ,, in *Enchantress*	2
BAXTER, Miss Laura ,,	1	BOSIO, Madame, *Martha*	1

PORTRAITS

DUMAS, Alexander, portrait 1
DUVERGER, Mdlle. ,, ... 4
DYAS, Miss Ada ,, ... 1
,, ,, vignette......... 1
,, ,, Titania 1
,, ,, Louis XI. 1
,, ,, Page 1

EBURNE, Mr. W. H., portrait...... 1
EBURNE, Miss M. ,, ... 2
ELSWORTHY, Miss ,, ... 3
,, ,, vignette 1
,, ,, Queen, Hamlet 2
,, ,, Lady Macbeth 1
,, ,, Lady Townley 1
EMDEN, Mrs., portrait............... 1
,, ,, Head of the Family 1
,, ,, Alfred the Great ... 1
,, ,, French Peasant ... 1
EMERY, Mr. S., Danny Man 2
ENNIS, Miss, portrait 1
EVERADI, Signor ,, ... 1

FARREN, Mr. W., portraits......... 2
FAUCIT, Miss Helen ,, ... 2
,, ,, Antigone ... 1
FAURE, M., portraits 2
FAUST & MARGUERITE (apotheosis)
ports. of Miss C. LECLERCQ, &c. 1
FECHTER, Mr., portraits............ 8
,, ,, Hamlet 10
,, ,, with the Ghost ... 2
,, ,, ,, Gravedigger 2
,, ,, Ruy Blas 4
,, ,, with Walter Lacy 6
,, ,, comic head......... 1
,, ,, medallion 1
,, ,, Hamlet, medallion 1
,, ,, comic head......... 1
FERNANDEZ, Mr. ,, ... 1
FISHER, Mr. David, portraits...... 5
,, ,, Dead Heart... 1
FITZCLARENCE, Miss, portrait...... 1
FITZWILLIAM, Mrs. E. ,, ... 1
FLORENCE, Mr. ,, ... 1
,, ,, in character 3
FLORENCE, Mrs. ,, ... 1
,, Mr. & Mrs. 1
FORMES, Herr 2

GALER, Mr. Elliot, portrait 1
GARCIA, Signor ,, ... 1
GARDONI, Signor ,, ... 6
,, ,, comic portrait... 1

PORTRAITS

GARIBALDI EXCURSIONISTS (Prin-
cess's Ballet)..................... 1
GASSIER, M., portraits............ 3
,, ,, Huguenots 1
,. ,, Lucrezia Borgia 1
GASSIER, Madame, portrait......... 1
GIUGLINI, Signor ,, ... 6
,, ,, comic portrait 1
,, ,, Il Ballo 1
GLUCK, portrait 1
GODDARD, Miss A., portraits...... 3
GORDON, Mr. W. ,, ... 1
,, ,, Tom Noddy's Secret 1
GRAHAM, Mr., portrait............. 1
GRAZIANI, Signor, portraits 3
,, ,, comic portraits 2
GRISI, Madame, portraits 3
,, ,, ,, comic... 1
GRISI & MARIO ,, ... 1
GUERRABELLA, Madame 2
GUINNESS, Miss 1

HAIGH, Mr. H., portrait 1
HALL, Mrs. S. C. ,, ... 1
HALLE, Mr. C. ,, ... 2
HANDEL ,, ... 1
HARRIS, Mr. A. ,, ... 1
HARRIS, Miss Maria, portraits ... 2
,, ,, Don Cæsar 2
HARRISON, Mr. W., portraits...... 3
HATTON, Mr. J. L. ,, ... 1
HAYDN ,, ... 1
HAYDON, Miss F. ,, ... 2
,, ,, in the Love Chase 2
,, ,, medallion 1
,, Misses F. and M. 1
,, Miss Maud 1
HAYES, Miss Catherine, portraits 2
HAYMARKET BALLET, Miller & Men 1
HEATH, Miss, portraits 4
,, ,, Lady of Lyons ... 2
,, ,, Fool's Revenge ... 3
,, ,, Viola 1
,, ,, Ophelia 2
,, ,, ,, medallion 1
,, ,, vignette 1
HENDERSON, Miss 1
HERAUD, Mr., portrait 1
HERAUD, Miss ,, ... 1
HERBERT, Miss ., ...11
,, ,, Isle of St. Tropez 5
,, ,, Up at the Hills... 2
,, ,, Endymion......... 2

ELEGANT MOROCCO ALBUMS FOR THE SMALL PORTRAITS,
Superbly gilt, with massive clasps,

	£	s.	d.			£	s.	d.
To contain 20 Portraits	0	5	0	To contain 100 Portraits		0	15	0
„ 30 „	0	7	6	200 „		2	0	0
„ 50 „	0	10	0					

With the Edges elaborately embossed, from 5s. to 15s. extra.

BEAUTIFUL FULL-LENGTH LARGE SIZE
PORTRAITS
OF

M. FECHTER (*Ruy Blas*); WALTER LACY (*Sallust*); ROBSON (*Porter's Knot*); A. WIGAN (portrait, and in *Isle of St. Tropez*); H. WIGAN (*Porter's Knot*); MISS HERBERT (*Up at the Hills*):

At 7s. 6d. each, or coloured, 15s. each.

A Medium size at 5s., or coloured, 10s. each.

MISS KATE CARSON (*Aladdin*); MISS HERBERT (*Isle of St. Tropez*); MR. ROBSON (portrait); MR. ROGERS (portrait); MDLLE. PATTI; MR. FECHTER (3 *as Hamlet*); MRS. CHARLES MATHEWS; MR. SIMS REEVES; MR. W. HARRISON; MISS L. PYNE; MISS F. HUDDART; MDLLE. TITIENS; SIGNOR GUIGLINI; MRS. C. YOUNG, &c., &c.

A CABINET SERIES OF HALF-LENGTH PORTRAITS
At 3s. 6d. each.

MISS KATE KELLY; MISS COTTRELL; MISS SEDGWICK; MR. F. MATTHEWS; MRS. F. MATTHEWS; DR. and MRS. PARKES; MR. C. YOUNG; MISS K. HICKSON; SIGNOR PICCO; MADAME CELESTE (*Miami*, and portrait); MISS FANNY REEVES; MR. WHARTON; MR. J. ROUSE; MR. G. HONEY; MR. ELLIOT GALER; MR. ST. ALBYN; MR. H. HAIGH; MISS MANDELBERT; MISS THIRLWALL; MISS CLEVELAND (*Conrad*); MISS ELSWORTHY, 2s. 6d.; SIGNOR TAGLIAFICO, 2s. 6d.; MISS HEATH (*Ophelia*), 2s. 6d.; MR. KEELEY, 2s. 6d.; MR. WIDDICOMBE, 2s. 6d.; MR. W. H. CHIPPENDALE, 2s. 6d.; &c.

FOUR FINE
SHAKESPERIAN PHOTOGRAPHS OF STRATFORD-ON-AVON,
One Shilling each.

PHOTOGRAPHS OF THE PRINCIPAL DRAMATIC ARTISTS,
In Costume, 1s. 6d. each.

PRINTED BY THOMAS SCOTT, WARWICK COURT, HOLBORN.

www.ingramcontent.com/pod-product-compliance
Lightning Source LLC
Chambersburg PA
CBHW032134080426
42733CB00008B/1063